Overcoming
Loneliness, Abandonment
& Depression

A Caregiver's Guide

Overcoming Loneliness, Abandonment & Depression
A Caregiver's Guide

Copyright © 2024
Ronald Lee Moore, Sr.

Printed in the United States of America

Cover design and book layout
One Creative Mind, LLC, publisher

ISBN: 979-8-9905229-7-8

Dedication

To all the caregivers who carry this immense
responsibility, often doing it alone and
without support.

When feelings of loneliness, abandonment,
or depression begin to creep in, please remember
that you are not alone in this journey. We stand
with you, sharing in the challenges and triumphs.
Your efforts and sacrifices are truly valued.

Caregivers DO Matter.

"There are only four kinds of people in the world,

Those who have been *caregivers*.

Those who are currently *caregivers*.

Those who will be *caregivers*,

and those who will need a *caregiver*.

— *Rosalynn Carter*

Contents

INTRODUCTION

Caregiving is a journey that demands immense strength and resilience, and it is certainly not for the faint of heart. The role of a caregiver often brings with it a whirlwind of unexpected, intimidating, and alarming situations that can arise out of nowhere, leaving you reeling. Just when you think you've found your footing, the rug is pulled out from beneath you, and you're thrust into yet another crisis. It's a relentless cycle that can leave you feeling overwhelmed, isolated, and, all too often, alone in your struggles.

When you step into the role of the primary caregiver, those who once shared the responsibilities often breathe a sigh of relief, grateful that someone is there to take the reins. However, as time passes, you may notice that those same individuals gradually, or sometimes abruptly, drift away. They may not mean to abandon you, but the reality is that you are often left to navigate this challenging path alone—untrained, unprepared, and yet shouldering an enormous responsibility.

This abrupt shift can give rise to feelings of loneliness and abandonment that creep in during your quiet moments, accompanied by an overwhelming sense of depression. Your social circle begins to shrink, and the phone calls that once brought joy and connection become infrequent. You may find it increasingly difficult to step outside your home, not just physically but emotionally. The demands of caregiving can be all-consuming, leaving little room for self-care or social interaction. In an effort to fill that void, you may turn to online shopping—Amazon Prime becomes your lifeline, delivering everything from necessary clothing to batteries for the television remote, and even indulgent snacks like dark chocolate to soothe your aching heart.

"REMEMBER THAT YOU ARE WORTHY OF CARE AND COMPASSION TOO."

Like many caregivers, you may find solace in your tablet, carrying it with you throughout the day, watching shows or movies while washing dishes or stealing a fleeting moment of respite in the bathroom. This constant companionship with a screen is a bittersweet comfort, providing distraction but also highlighting the isolation that permeates your life.

It's crucial to understand that being alone and experiencing loneliness are two distinct experiences. Yes, you may be physically alone in your caregiving duties, but loneliness is a deeper emotional wound—the sensation that no one is truly there for you, that no one comprehends the daily struggles you face. This feeling can quickly morph into a profound sense of abandonment, especially in moments of crisis when you find yourself cleaning up after an accident or responding to urgent needs.

As the days, weeks, and months roll on, these emotions can spiral into desolation, leading to a pervasive misery that can feel all-encompassing. It's a heartbreaking reality that many caregivers endure, often unnoticed or unacknowledged by those around them. Yet through it all, the obligations to your loved ones remain steadfast, demanding your attention even when your own emotional well-being is hanging by a thread.

But do not despair. Even when the world feels heavy and dark, know that there is help available, even if it seems elusive. You are not alone in this silent struggle. As you continue to navigate this complex and often painful journey, we invite you to explore this guide further. Within its pages, you may discover comfort, encouragement, and solutions that can help illuminate your path, reminding you that there is hope amidst the chaos. Reach out, seek support, and remember that you are worthy of care and compassion too. *Caregivers DO Matter!*

CHAPTER 1 — LONELINESS

Loneliness is a subjective feeling of sadness, emptiness, and isolation resulting from a lack of satisfying social connections or meaningful relationships with others. It can be experienced even when one is surrounded by others or in a crowded place. Loneliness is often accompanied by a sense of disconnection or alienation from others and a feeling of being misunderstood or unappreciated. It can have negative effects on a person's mental and physical health, and can lead to depression, anxiety, and other psychological and emotional problems.

Caregiving is a challenging job, whether you're taking care of an aging parent, disabled child, or a sick spouse. It can be rewarding to help improve someone's life, but it can also be draining and isolating. Full-time caregivers, in particular, face a unique set of challenges, including financial strain, constant worry, and a lack of social interaction. These challenges can lead to feelings of loneliness and depression.

Causes of Loneliness in Full-Time Caregivers

Loneliness is the result of a lack of social interaction and feelings of disconnection. Full-time caregivers are more susceptible to feelings of loneliness due to their limited mobility and social isolation. Some of the causes of loneliness in caregivers include:

Financial Strain: Full-time caregiving can cause financial stress, as it often results in lost wages or decreased employment opportunities. The financial strain can affect a caregiver's mental health, leading to feelings of loneliness and isolation.

Lack of Social Interaction: Caregivers often have limited opportunities for social interaction, as they spend most of their time caring for their loved ones. Their social life may revolve around their caregiving responsibilities, causing them to feel isolated and disconnected from their peers.

Burnout: Caregivers who experience burnout may feel emotionally and physically exhausted, leading to a lack of motivation to engage in social activities outside of their caregiving responsibilities. This can result in feelings of loneliness and isolation.

Effects of Loneliness in Caregivers

Loneliness can have serious negative effects on a caregiver's mental and physical health, including:

Depression: Caregivers who experience loneliness may develop depression. The lack of social interaction and feelings of isolation can result in sadness, hopelessness, and a lack of motivation.

Reduced Quality of Life: Loneliness can affect a caregiver's overall quality of life. The lack of social interaction and feelings of disconnection can lead to decreased enjoyment in activities, a diminished sense of purpose, and a lack of fulfillment.

Physical Health Issues: Loneliness can also negatively affect a caregiver's physical health. The stress and emotional toll of caregiving can lead to chronic health problems, such as high blood pressure, heart disease, and a weakened immune system.

"It's Okay to Ask for Help"

Judith had always been "the life of the party." With her infectious smile and bubbly personality, she was the friend everyone wanted to have around. "She was always the first to organize a night out," and her phone would buzz incessantly with messages from friends inviting her for drinks or a movie. Laughter and joy seemed to follow her wherever she went, and she thrived on the energy of her social life.

However, everything changed dramatically when her mother was diagnosed with dementia. Judith had always shared a close bond with her mother; they were more than just family—they were best friends. Faced with the reality of her mother's condition, Judith made a heart-wrenching decision. She quit her job, leaving behind her career, her colleagues, and the bustling life she once knew. "I moved in with my mother," she recalled, "determined to give her the best care possible."

At first, the transition felt noble, even empowering. Judith immersed herself in her role as a caregiver, learning everything she could about dementia and how to support her mother's needs. Yet, as the months turned into years, Judith found herself becoming "increasingly isolated."

Initially, her friends reached out, genuinely concerned for her well-being. But as time passed, the calls and texts dwindled. They didn't understand the toll that caring for someone with dementia was taking on her. Judith felt as if she were trapped in a bubble, her world shrinking while her friends continued their lives. "I was exhausted all the time," she admitted, "barely getting any sleep at night." The weight of caregiving pressed down on her, and she found it difficult to maintain her former social life.

The once lively house became eerily quiet, punctuated only by the occasional outbursts from her mother. Judith's phone rarely rang anymore; when it did, it was often a telemarketer's call—a stark reminder of how disconnected she had become. "I felt like I was living in a completely different world," she reflected, "one where my friends were still going out, having fun, and enjoying life."

Judith made attempts to keep in touch with her friends, but conversations felt strained. "I had less and less to talk about," she confessed. Her days revolved around caring for her mother, leaving little room for anything else. She felt as if she were losing touch not only with her friends but with herself. The vibrant woman who had once filled rooms with laughter now felt invisible and unheard.

As the years progressed, her mother's condition worsened. Judith faced an uphill battle as her mother became increasingly aggressive and violent, making caregiving even more challenging. The physical and emotional toll began to manifest in Judith herself; she was constantly exhausted, her nerves frayed. "I found it hard to cope with the overwhelming sense of loneliness that surrounded me," she admitted, her voice heavy with the weight of her experiences.

"IT FELT GOOD TO RECLAIM PARTS OF MYSELF THAT I THOUGHT I HAD LOST FOREVER."

Then came the day when Judith's mother passed away. It was a moment filled with devastating sorrow, yet oddly tinged with relief. Judith had devoted herself to caring for her mother for so long that the thought of life without her was daunting. "I had been her caretaker for years," she said quietly, "and I didn't know how to be anything else."

After the funeral, Judith found herself grappling with an emptiness that felt insurmountable. She knew she had to rebuild her life, to reclaim her identity beyond that of a caregiver. She reached out to her old friends, hoping to reconnect, to find solace in shared memories and laughter. But what she discovered was heartbreaking. "They had all moved on with their lives," she realized. Her friends were now married, some with children and flourishing careers. They had responsibilities that kept them busy, leaving little time for Judith and her lingering grief.

Judith felt more alone than ever before. She had not only lost her mother but also her friends and, in many ways, her sense of purpose. "It was as if I had been left behind," she reflected, "watching others live their lives while I felt stuck in my own sorrow." The loneliness was suffocating, wrapping around her like a heavy blanket that she couldn't shake off.

In the days that followed, Judith found herself wandering through her empty house, filled with echoes of laughter and memories that now seemed distant. She would sit in her mother's favorite chair, staring out the window, wondering how to move forward. "I didn't know if I even wanted to," she admitted. The thought of reconnecting with the world felt daunting, almost impossible.

Yet, somewhere deep inside, a flicker of determination began to emerge. Judith realized that she had to take small steps. "I didn't want to feel this lonely anymore," she thought resolutely. So, she started by reaching out to a local support group for caregivers. It was there that she met others who had experienced similar losses, who understood the complexities of grief and loneliness.

Slowly, Judith began to share her story, her feelings, and her fears. She learned that vulnerability could be a bridge, connecting her to others who had navigated the choppy waters of caregiving and loss. Through shared experiences, she found solace, laughter, and, gradually, the courage to re-enter the world outside her home.

With time, Judith began to reconnect with her passions—the arts, gardening, and even the occasional night out. "It felt good to reclaim parts of myself that I thought I had lost forever," she reflected with a newfound sense of hope.

Though the journey was far from over, Judith realized that loneliness does not have to be a permanent state. It can be a chapter in a much larger story—one of resilience, healing, and rediscovery. "I learned that it's okay to ask for help," she said, a smile breaking through her solemn expression. "And that sometimes, it takes losing everything to find a way back to yourself."

Signs of Loneliness in Caregivers

Identifying the signs of loneliness in caregivers can be crucial in preventing its negative effects. Some of the signs of loneliness in caregivers include:

MANAGING LONELINESS IS AN ONGOING PROCESS FOR CAREGIVERS.

Fatigue: Feeling tired or exhausted despite getting enough sleep can be a sign of loneliness. Caregivers who feel lonely may have no energy or motivation to engage in activities outside of their caregiving responsibilities.

Social Isolation: If a caregiver is not participating in social activities or spends most of their time alone, they may be experiencing social isolation.

Feelings of Sadness or Depression: Caregivers who are feeling lonely may experience feelings of sadness or depression. They may feel hopeless, unmotivated, and struggle to find joy in activities they once enjoyed.

Overcoming Loneliness in Caregivers: Overcoming loneliness in caregivers can take time and effort, but it is possible. Here are some ways caregivers can overcome loneliness:

Seek Social Support: Joining a support group, engaging in online communities, or attending social events can provide an opportunity for caregivers to connect with others who understand their experiences.

Take Care of Yourself

Practicing self-care can reduce stress and improve overall well-being. Caregivers should prioritize their physical and emotional health by eating well, exercising regularly, and finding time for activities they enjoy.

Reach Out for Help

Caregivers can ask for help from friends, family, or community resources to reduce their caregiving responsibilities and create more time for social interaction.

Results Over Time

Managing loneliness is an ongoing process for caregivers. The strategies mentioned can help alleviate loneliness in the short-term, but caregivers must continue to seek social support and prioritize self-care to maintain mental and physical well-being in the long term.

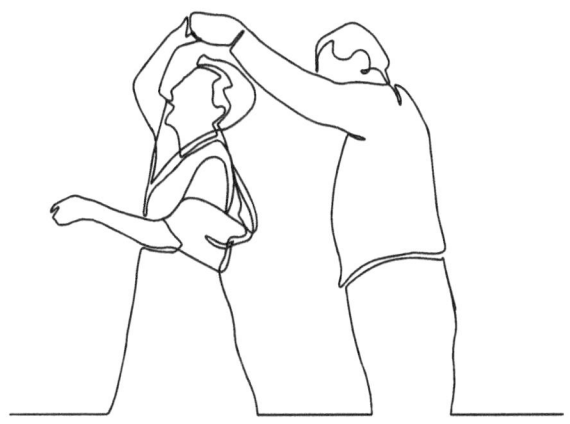

No Longer Lonely

Anita always understood that being a full-time caregiver for her mother, Deana, would be a complex and demanding role. Deana, a single mother, became completely deaf shortly after Anita was born. From that moment on, she relied entirely on her daughter for everything—from basic needs to emotional support. Living in the quiet, isolated rural area of Edenton, North Carolina, with few visitors or relatives, Anita's only daily company was her mother.

As the years passed, Anita found herself grappling with an overwhelming sense of loneliness. She rarely left the house, venturing out only for essential errands or to take Deana to medical appointments.

"I love my mom, I really do," Anita often reminded herself, "but sometimes I just wish I had someone to talk to who wasn't dependent on me." The longing for a relationship, for companionship beyond the walls of her home, gnawed at her. But the stark reality of their situation made any hope of that feel impossible.

When winter arrived, it brought with it not just the snow but an even deeper sense of isolation. The white blanket that covered the ground mirrored the solitude that enveloped Anita. Cabin fever set in, and she found herself talking to herself out loud in the empty rooms of their house. "What's wrong with me?" she would mutter, shaking her head. "I'm talking to myself like a crazy person." She knew it wasn't healthy, but the silence was deafening, and she craved any form of interaction.

Desperate for a connection to humanity, Anita turned to the internet. She began spending hours scrolling through social media, reading blogs, and watching videos. Yet, no matter how engaging these distractions were, they could not fill the void she felt. "I need something real," she thought. "I need someone to understand what I'm going through."

One fateful day, she stumbled upon an online forum specifically for caregivers. At first, doubt crept in. "What if they don't get me?" she thought, hesitating to sign up. But after a few moments of contemplation, she decided to give it a try. With a mix of nervousness and hope, she introduced herself and shared her story. "Hi, I'm Anita," she typed, her fingers trembling over the keyboard. "I care for my mother, who is deaf, and sometimes I feel so alone."

To her surprise, the response was overwhelming. Within minutes, messages flooded in from complete strangers offering words of encouragement and support. "You're not alone in this, Anita," one user wrote. "We're all in the same boat." Others shared their own experiences, recounting the challenges they faced as caregivers. "I get it," another user commented. "It can feel so isolating. But we're here for you."

As the days turned into weeks, Anita found herself spending more and more time on the forum. She developed friendships with fellow caregivers, and they discussed everything from the daily struggles of caregiving to their hopes and dreams for the future. "I never thought I could make friends online," Anita admitted in a chat one evening. "But this has been a lifeline for me."

Over time, the connections she formed began to change her outlook. She felt a weight lifting off her shoulders, replaced by a sense of belonging. "I can't believe how much I've been missing this," she reflected. "Talking to people who really understand— it's incredible."

Despite her newfound community, Anita never neglected her responsibilities as a caregiver. Each day, she continued to care for Deana with unwavering love and dedication. "Mom, I'm here for you," she would say, brushing her mother's hair back gently. "You're my priority." But now, whenever she faced a difficult day or felt overwhelmed, she had a virtual support system to turn to.

As the snow melted and spring arrived, Anita experienced a profound realization. She had overcome her loneliness in a way she never expected. "I'm not just talking to myself anymore," she thought, smiling at the thought of her online friends. Instead, she was engaging with a group of people who truly understood her struggles and were there to support her through them.

"WE CAN FACE ANYTHING TOGETHER."

One evening, as she prepared dinner for Deana, she found herself reflecting on how much her life had changed. "I still have tough days," she said to herself, stirring a pot on the stove. "But I also have friends who care." She felt a joy she hadn't experienced in years, a sense of hope that things could improve.

Anita knew that caring for her mother would always be a challenging task, but she was no longer alone. The community of caregivers she had found became not just a support network but a group of friends who had enriched her life. "We can face anything together," she typed in a message one night. "Thank you all for being there for me."

With a renewed sense of purpose, Anita embraced the challenges ahead. She felt empowered, knowing that no matter what difficulties she faced, she had a community of understanding friends to lean on. "I can do this," she whispered to herself, feeling a warmth in her heart. "I'm not just a caregiver; I'm part of something bigger."

And so, as the days grew longer and brighter with the arrival of spring, Anita stepped into her role with a newfound positivity. She was no longer just a lone caregiver in a quiet house; she was part of a vibrant community, and for the first time in a long time, she felt truly connected to humanity.

How to Handle Loneliness as a Caregiver

Handling loneliness as a caregiver can be challenging, but there are ways to manage it. Here are some tips for caregivers:

Recognize that Loneliness is Normal: Loneliness is a common experience for caregivers. Recognizing that it's normal to feel lonely can help caregivers take steps to manage these feelings.

Prioritize Self-Care: Taking care of oneself should be a top priority for caregivers. Self-care can include physical exercise, engaging in hobbies, or seeking professional support.

Take Advantage of Technology: Smart phones, computers, and other devices can provide a way for caregivers to connect with others virtually. Social media, video chats, and online gaming can help caregivers stay connected to their friends and family.

Finally, loneliness can be a difficult feeling to manage, and it's especially challenging for full-time caregivers. However, by recognizing the signs and causes of loneliness and taking practical steps to manage it, caregivers can prioritize their emotional and physical well-being. Remember to seek social support, practice self-care, and take advantage of technology to stay connected to friends and family.

Frequently Asked Questions:

Is it normal for caregivers to feel lonely?

Yes, loneliness is a common experience among caregivers, especially those who provide full-time care.

What are some ways to prevent loneliness in full-time caregivers?

Seeking social support, making time for self-care and leisure activities, and practicing stress-reducing techniques can help prevent loneliness in full-time caregivers.

Can loneliness in full-time caregivers lead to depression?

Yes, loneliness can increase the risk of depression and other mental health issues in full-time caregivers.

What resources are available to help caregivers overcome loneliness?

Support groups, respite care, and professional counseling or therapy are all resources that can help caregivers overcome loneliness.

How can I find a caregiver support group?

You can search for caregiver support groups in your area through websites like AARP.

Chapter 2 — Abandonment

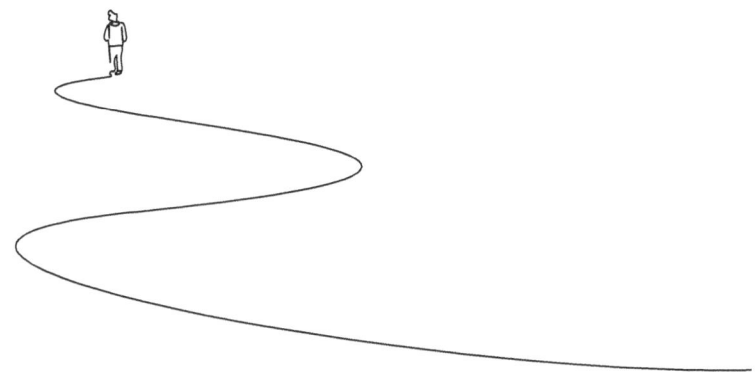

The feeling of being abandoned or experiencing abandonment according to full-time caregivers can be described as a sense of isolation or being left alone to manage the responsibilities of caregiving without sufficient support or resources.

Caregivers may feel overwhelmed, unsupported, and emotionally drained, as they often have to sacrifice their own needs and desires to provide care for their loved ones. These feelings can be intensified when caregivers feel that their efforts are not recognized or appreciated by others and when they lack access to adequate resources such as respite care, counseling, or financial support.

Overall, the feeling of abandonment can be a significant source of stress and emotional burden for full-time caregivers, and it is important for them to seek out support to prevent burnout.

These feelings may arise due to a variety of factors, including the caregiver feeling like they are not receiving enough support or recognition for their efforts, or feeling like they are carrying the burden of caregiving alone.

Here are some ways that feelings of abandonment can present them-selves in caregiving, as well as some strategies for managing these feelings:

Emotional distance: Caregivers may feel emotionally distant from their loved one, particularly if their loved one is unable to express gratitude or appreciation for the care they are receiving.

Social isolation: Caregivers may feel socially isolated if they are unable to participate in social activities or if they feel like they cannot leave their loved one alone.

Resentment: Caregivers may feel resentful toward family members or friends who are not helping with caregiving responsibilities, leading to feelings of abandonment.

Burnout: Caregivers may experience burnout if they feel like they are carrying the burden of caregiving alone, leading to feelings of exhaustion and emotional depletion.

EVEN WHEN THE CAREGIVER IS NOT ABANDONED, OFTEN THE FEELINGS OF ABANDONMENT SURFACE.

Reasons A Caregiver May Be Abandoned

Often one who becomes the sole caregiver may be abandoned by the rest of the family. Some reasons include:

Lack of awareness: Some family members may not fully under-stand the extent of care that is required for the person in need, or they may not understand the burden that the sole caregiver is facing.

Distance: Family members who live far away from the person in need may not be able to provide physical support and may not fully appreciate the challenges of caregiving from a distance.

Personal issues: Family members may have their own personal issues or commitments that prevent them from providing the necessary support, or they may have strained relationships with the caregiver or the person in need.

Lack of resources: Some family members may not have the financial or other resources to provide support, or they may not have access to the necessary resources to help the caregiver.

Burnout: Caregiving can be emotionally and physically exhausting, and some family members may feel overwhelmed and unable to provide the necessary support.

It's important to note that every family is unique, and there may be other factors at play that contribute to why some family members may abandon the sole caregiver. It's important for families to communicate openly and honestly about their needs and limitations, and to work together to provide the best possible care for their loved ones.

Even when the caregiver is not abandoned, often the feelings of abandonment surface. It can happen when the caregiver feels burned out or overwhelmed by the demands of caregiving, or when they feel that they are not appreciated or valued. It can also happen when the caregiver is dealing with their own personal problems or when they feel that their efforts are not making a difference.

Whatever the cause, abandonment is a serious issue for both the caregiver and the person they are caring for. It can lead to feelings of guilt, anxiety, and depression, and it can also impact the quality of care that the caregiver is able to provide.

Signs of Abandonment

There are several signs that a full-time caregiver may be experiencing abandonment.

These include:

- Feeling overwhelmed or unable to cope
- Feeling like nobody appreciates their efforts
- Feeling guilty or ashamed about their role as a caregiver
- Becoming impatient or irritable with the person they are caring for
- Feeling resentful of the person they are caring for
- Neglecting their own self-care, such as not eating properly or not getting enough sleep.

If you are a full-time caregiver and you are experiencing any of these signs, it is important to seek help.

Abandoned, Yet Still Committed

Sometimes, the heart loves so deeply that it forgets to take care of itself." This thought echoed in Gregory's mind as he sat in the dim light of the living room, the soft hum of the television barely registering. His grandfather, Arthur, was dozing in the armchair across from him, a quilt draped over his frail body. Gregory had always felt a deep connection with Arthur, forged through countless hours of shared stories and laughter. But as the years passed, that bond was tested in ways he never anticipated.

In those early days, Gregory would often reminisce about their adventures together. "Remember the time we went fishing at Lake Willow?" Gregory would say with a chuckle, and Arthur's eyes would twinkle with nostalgia as he replied, "You caught that big trout while I was busy untangling my line!" They would share laughs, the kind that warmed the heart and made the world seem brighter.

But as Arthur aged, their conversations began to shift. The laughter became punctuated with pauses filled with concern. "Gregory, I need your help with some things," Arthur would say, his voice tinged with a vulnerability that tugged at Gregory's heartstrings. It started with small tasks—picking up groceries or driving Arthur to his doctor's appointments. Gregory didn't mind; it felt good to help.

"I NEED YOU HERE WITH ME, NOT JUST PHYSICALLY, BUT EMOTIONALLY."

However, as the months rolled on, those small tasks escalated into a full-time job. "I can't keep up with this," Gregory confessed to his best friend, Jake, one evening over cold beers on the porch. "It's like every day there's something new. Bathing, dressing, medications… it never ends."

Jake nodded, his expression serious. "It's a lot, man. You need to take care of yourself too."

Gregory didn't fully grasp the weight of those words until it became his reality. With every passing week, Arthur's condition deteriorated, leaving Gregory feeling like a soldier in a relentless battle. "I'm doing my best, Grandpa," he would say, trying to mask the exhaustion in his voice. "I promise." But underneath his resolute exterior, he was crumbling.

His wife, Lily, initially supportive, began to withdraw as the demands of caregiving intensified. "Gregory, I feel like I'm losing you," she said one night, her voice trembling. "You're always so focused on your grandfather. What about us?"

"I'm trying to help him, Lily!" Gregory snapped back, a hint of desperation in his tone. "He needs me!"

"And what about what we need?" Lily's eyes filled with tears. "I can't do this alone. I need you here with me, not just physically, but emotionally."

Days turned into weeks, and the tension between them escalated. One evening, as they sat at the dinner table, Lily finally broke down. "I can't do this anymore, Gregory. I'm leaving." Her words cut through the air like a knife, and for a moment, time stood still.

"Please, don't say that," Gregory pleaded, his heart racing. "I can make it work. We can make it work."

"I need to focus on myself," she replied firmly, her resolve unyielding. "I can't be your support system while I'm drowning." And with that, she packed her things and left, leaving Gregory feeling abandoned and heartbroken.

As the days turned into a blur of caregiving, Gregory felt the isolation creep in. Family members who had promised to help seemed to vanish when he needed them the most. "I just need a little support," he would say during phone calls that ended in hollow promises. "I can't do this all alone." But the reality was that he was alone, grappling with the emotional and physical weight of his grandfather's care.

"You're doing a great job, Gregory," a nurse at the clinic told him one day as she checked Arthur's vitals. "It's not easy, but you're handling it."

"Thanks, but I feel like I'm drowning," Gregory admitted, his voice barely above a whisper. "I don't know how much longer I can keep this up."

Just when it seemed that all hope was lost, Gregory discovered online caregiver support groups. "You're not alone," one member wrote in a forum. "There are others out there struggling just like you." It was a revelation. He began to connect with other caregivers, sharing stories and advice, finding solace in their shared experiences.

"I didn't think I would find friends this way," he shared with a fellow caregiver named Sarah during one of their video calls. "But it feels good to talk to someone who understands."

"Absolutely," Sarah replied, her smile warm and inviting. "You need to remember that taking care of yourself is just as important as taking care of your grandfather. Caregivers do matter."

Gregory took those words to heart. He began to carve out time for himself, whether it was a quiet walk in the park or a few moments with a good book. It wasn't much, but it was a start.

As weeks turned into months, Gregory became more adept at managing his responsibilities. He learned to set boundaries, to ask for help when he needed it, and to prioritize his own well-being. "I can't pour from an empty cup," he reminded himself, echoing the advice he had received from his newfound friends.

"Grandpa," he said one afternoon while helping Arthur with his lunch, "I've been talking to some people online, and they've really helped me see that I can't do this alone."

Arthur looked up, his eyes filled with understanding. "You're a good man, Gregory. Sometimes, it's okay to lean on others. I've had my share of help in my life."

Those words struck a chord. Gregory realized that he didn't have to shoulder the burden alone. Slowly, he reached out to family again, explaining his struggles and seeking their assistance.

As the seasons changed, so did Gregory's approach to caregiving. He remained committed to Arthur, but he no longer neglected his own needs. He found joy in the little things—an afternoon spent gardening with Arthur or cooking their favorite meals together. "Let's make your famous stew, Grandpa," Gregory would say, laughter filling the kitchen as they diced vegetables side by side.

Even during the toughest days, he found strength in the community he had built. "You're doing an amazing job," Sarah would text him during particularly overwhelming days. "Remember, you're not alone."

Eventually, Arthur's health began to decline further, and Gregory found himself facing difficult decisions. "What do you want, Grandpa?" he asked one evening, sitting beside him on the bed. "I want you to be happy, but I need to know what you want."

"You've done enough for me, Gregory," Arthur whispered, his voice tinged with gratitude. "Whatever you decide, just know that I love you."

As Gregory navigated the complexities of caregiving, he learned invaluable lessons about love, sacrifice, and the importance of self-care. The journey was challenging, filled with moments of doubt and pain, but it was also rich with connection and understanding.

"Abandonment can be a heavy burden," he reflected one evening, gazing at the stars from his porch. "But commitment, even in the face of adversity, can light the way."

Ultimately, Gregory found peace in his role as a caregiver, understanding that even when he felt abandoned, he could still be committed. His journey with Arthur was not just about duty; it became a testament to the enduring power of love. And in that love, he discovered the strength to keep going, no matter the challenges that lay ahead.

CAREGIVERS WHO FEEL ABANDONED MAY EXPERIENCE A RANGE OF NEGATIVE EMOTIONS,.

Caregiving can be an overwhelming and exhausting experience, especially when it feels like you're doing it alone.

If Gregory feels abandoned by his family, it may be helpful for him to reach out to them and express his feelings. It's possible that they simply don't realize how much he is struggling and may be willing to offer more support if they understand the gravity of the situation. Alternatively, there may be reasons why they are unable to help, such as work or other family commitments.

In addition to reaching out to his family, Gregory may also want to consider seeking support from outside sources. There are many organizations and resources available to caregivers that can provide guidance, advice, and emotional support.

For example, the National Alliance for Caregiving offers a wealth of resources for caregivers, including support groups and educational materials.

Finally, it's important for Gregory to take care of his own well-being as well as that of his grandfather. Caregiver burnout is a real risk, and it's essential for Gregory to take breaks and find ways to recharge his batteries. This may mean taking advantage of respite care services, asking friends or neighbors for help, or simply taking some time for himself to relax and recharge.

It's important to note that abandoning a caregiver can have serious consequences for the person receiving care. If you are a caregiver who is struggling, it's important to reach out for help and support before making any decisions about stopping care.

Feelings of abandonment can have a significant impact on caregivers, who are often responsible for providing ongoing care and support to others. Caregivers who feel abandoned may experience a range of negative emotions, such as anxiety, depression, anger, and resentment. They may also feel overwhelmed and stressed, particularly if they feel they are solely responsible for providing care and support.

In some cases, caregivers may feel abandoned by the person they are caring for, particularly if that person is unable to express gratitude or appreciation for the care they are receiving. Caregivers may also feel abandoned by family members or friends who are not providing the support or assistance they need.

Feelings of abandonment can also lead to caregiver burnout, a state of physical, emotional, and mental exhaustion that can result from prolonged stress and the demands of caregiving. Caregiver burnout can cause a range of symptoms, such as fatigue, irritability, and decreased motivation.

If you are a full-time caregiver and you feel like you are experiencing abandonment, it is important to act.

LONELINESS AND ABANDONMENT ARE OFTEN INTERTWINED EMOTIONS.

Some strategies that may be helpful include:

- Seeking help from a mental health professional
- Prioritizing your own self-care needs
- Reaching out to family and friends for support
- Talking to the person you are caring for about your feelings
- Considering taking a break from your caregiving role if necessary.

Remember, abandonment is a serious issue, but with the right strategies and support in place, it is possible to overcome abandonment and continue to provide high-quality care to the person you are caring for. If you are experiencing abandonment, remember to prioritize your own needs and seek help when necessary.

What is the difference between the feeling of loneliness compared to feeling abandonment?

Loneliness and abandonment are two emotional states that can have profound effects on an individual's mental well-being. While they may seem similar at first glance, there are key differences between the two that are important to understand. In this comprehensive article, we will delve into the nuances of loneliness versus abandonment, explore real-life examples, and provide insights into how these feelings can impact individuals differently.

What is the difference between the feeling of loneliness compared to feeling abandonment?

Loneliness and abandonment are often intertwined emotions, but they stem from different sources. Loneliness typically occurs when a person feels disconnected or isolated from others, even when surrounded by people. On the other hand, abandonment is the feeling of being deserted or left behind by someone significant in one's life, leading to a sense of betrayal and neglect.

Examples of Loneliness:

1. A student sitting alone in the cafeteria, feeling unseen and ignored by classmates.

2. An elderly person living far from family members, longing for companionship and a listening ear.

Examples of Abandonment:

1. A child whose parent leaves them at a young age, feeling a deep sense of loss and rejection.

2. A partner who is suddenly ghosted by their significant other, experiencing emotional turmoil and insecurity.

Exploring Loneliness:

Loneliness is a complex emotion that can manifest in various situations and stages of life. It is not solely determined by external factors but also by one's internal perception of social connections and belongingness.

Understanding Abandonment:

Abandonment is often linked to feelings of betrayal, rejection, and unworthiness. It can have a lasting impact on an individual's self-esteem and ability to trust others.

Healing from Abandonment:

1. Self-Exploration: Reflecting on past experiences and understanding triggers can aid in healing from abandonment wounds.

2. Building Trust: Establishing healthy boundaries and fostering trusting relationships can help in overcoming abandonment fears.

Understanding the subtle distinctions between loneliness and abandonment is essential for effectively navigating the intricate landscape of human emotions. Although both feelings can lead to significant distress, they stem from different emotional experiences and necessitate unique approaches for healing and personal growth.

Loneliness often arises from a lack of social connection, while abandonment typically relates to feelings of rejection or loss. By identifying the underlying causes of these emotions and seeking the right support, individuals can take meaningful steps toward emotional well-being. This journey not only fosters healing but also promotes self-empowerment, enabling individuals to build healthier relationships and enhance their overall quality of life.

Frequently Asked Questions:

What is abandonment in full-time caregivers?

Abandonment in full-time caregivers occurs when the caregiver feels like they are on their own and unsupported, leading to negative effects on both the caregiver and the person they are caring for.

What are the causes of abandonment in full-time caregivers?

Abandonment may be caused by burnout, feeling unappreciated or undervalued, dealing with personal problems, or feeling like their efforts are not making a difference.

Can abandonment in full-time caregivers be overcome?

Yes, abandonment can be overcome through seeking emotional support, prioritizing self-care, setting boundaries, developing a support system, and keeping a positive mind-set.

How can loneliness affect mental health?

Loneliness has been linked to increased stress levels, depression, and anxiety. It can also affect physical health by weakening the immune system and disrupting sleep patterns.

Is abandonment always intentional?

Abandonment can be both intentional and unintentional. While some instances involve a deliberate decision to leave, others may result from circumstances beyond one's control.

Can loneliness lead to feelings of abandonment?

Yes, prolonged feelings of loneliness can sometimes morph into feelings of abandonment, especially when individuals believe they are being emotionally neglected or overlooked.

Are there different types of loneliness?

Yes, there are different types of loneliness: emotional loneliness (lack of close relationships), social loneliness (lack of social connections), and existential loneliness (feeling disconnected from a deeper purpose in life).

CHAPTER 3 — DEPRESSION

Depression is often characterized by a persistent sense of sadness or a profound loss of interest in activities that once brought joy. This emotional state can be accompanied by a variety of distressing symptoms, including alterations in sleep patterns, changes in appetite, feelings of worthlessness or guilt, difficulty concentrating, and, in severe cases, thoughts of death or suicide. Such experiences can be particularly pronounced among full-time caregivers, who may grapple not only with their own emotional struggles but also with overwhelming feelings of exhaustion and isolation.

Caregiving is an inherently demanding and stressful role. Caregivers often prioritize the needs of their loved ones above their own, which can lead to a neglect of self-care and personal well-being. This self-sacrifice, while noble, can result in chronic stress and ultimately contribute to feelings of burnout and depression. The emotional toll of constantly being in a caretaker role can create a sense of entrapment, where caregivers feel they have little to no time or energy to address their own mental health needs.

Depression is a serious mental health condition that transcends age, gender, and background, affecting individuals from all walks of life. Its impact can be profound, significantly impairing a person's quality of life, interpersonal relationships, and overall ability to function in daily activities. Beyond the emotional aspects, depression manifests through a myriad of physical symptoms, including changes in appetite and sleep disturbances, persistent fatigue, unexplained aches and pains, and difficulties in concentrating. Individuals may also experience an overwhelming sense of guilt or worthlessness, compounding their distress.

Recognizing the signs of depression is crucial, especially for caregivers who may be at heightened risk due to the demands of their role. It is essential for caregivers to seek support and establish boundaries that allow for self-care. By doing so, they can foster their own mental health and well-being, ultimately benefiting not only themselves but also those they care for. Addressing these challenges head-on is vital for improving both quality of life and emotional resilience.

"WE CAN FACE ANYTHING TOGETHER."

There are several types of depression, including major depressive disorder, persistent depressive disorder, seasonal affective disorder, and postpartum depression. Treatment for depression typically involves a combination of medication, therapy, lifestyle changes, or a combination of all.

Now, let's delve into a story about Edith who is caring for her fifteen-year-old daughter Roseanne

Defeating Depression

Edith gazed out the window, the morning light casting a warm glow over the kitchen. It was a beautiful day, yet the weight on her chest felt heavier than ever. "Mom, can you help me with my medicine?" Roseanne called from her bedroom, her voice breaking the silence.

"Of course, sweetheart!" Edith replied, forcing a smile as she made her way down the hallway. Roseanne's chronic illness had changed their lives irrevocably, and while Edith had embraced the role of caregiver, the toll it took on her was beginning to show.

At first, the challenges had seemed manageable. "I can do this," she had reassured herself. "I just need to stay organized." Edith had established a routine, meticulously scheduling Roseanne's medical appointments and managing her medications like a general preparing for battle. But as the months dragged on, the weight of responsibility became suffocating.

"Mom, I don't feel good again," Roseanne sighed, clutching her stomach as she lay back on her pillow. Edith rushed to her side, concern washing over her. "What's wrong, honey? Is it the medicine?"

"I think it's just... everything," Roseanne said, her eyes shimmering with unshed tears. "Sometimes it feels like it's never going to get better."

Edith's heart ached. "I know, love. But we're in this together. You're so strong," she encouraged, brushing a strand of hair from Roseanne's forehead. Yet, as she spoke the words, doubt crept in. Was she really strong? Was she doing enough?

Days turned into weeks, and each morning felt like waking up to a weight that pressed down harder than the last. As she juggled her job, Roseanne's needs, and household responsibilities, Edith found herself retreating from the world. "You should come to book club this week," her friend Laura suggested over the phone one evening.

"I can't, Laura. I have too much to do," Edith replied, her voice barely above a whisper.

"Edith, you need a break. You can't keep doing this alone," Laura urged.

"I'm fine," Edith insisted, but the truth was far from it. Each time she turned down an invitation, she felt more isolated. She could see the pity in her friends' eyes, and it made her feel worse.

Her own reflection had started to look foreign, the vibrant woman she once was replaced by someone who seemed tired and worn. "I can't even take care of myself," she muttered one afternoon as she stood before the mirror, her eyes hollow.

"I CAN'T KEEP PRETENDING I'M OKAY."

Finally, one evening, after a particularly challenging day, Edith found herself sitting on the floor of Roseanne's room, surrounded by scattered toys. Roseanne had fallen asleep, but the weight of her worries kept Edith wide awake. "What am I doing wrong?" she whispered into the stillness of the room.

As if in response, her phone buzzed. It was a message from Laura: "I'm here for you. Please talk to me." Tears welled in Edith's eyes. "I can't keep pretending I'm okay," she admitted aloud.

The next morning, she made a decision that changed everything. "I need help," she told Roseanne, her voice trembling. "I'm going to see a therapist."

Roseanne looked up, surprise etched on her face. "But Mom, you're always so strong. You don't need therapy."

"I'm strong because I'm asking for help," Edith said gently. "It's okay to need support."

With that, Edith took her first step toward healing. At her first therapy session, she felt vulnerable as she recounted her struggles. "I feel like I'm failing Roseanne," she confessed to Dr. Patel, her therapist. "No matter how hard I try, it's never enough."

Dr. Patel nodded empathetically. "It's common for caregivers to feel that way. But you must remember that your well-being is just as important as Roseanne's. You can't pour from an empty cup."

Edith absorbed the words, a flicker of hope igniting within her. "How do I stop feeling guilty?" she asked, her voice shaky.

"By acknowledging that you're human," Dr. Patel replied. "You're doing an incredible job, but that doesn't mean you shouldn't take care of yourself. What do you enjoy doing?"

Edith paused, the question catching her off guard. "I used to love painting," she said slowly.

"Then let's find a way to bring that back into your life," Dr. Patel encouraged. "Art can be a powerful outlet for your emotions."

With each session, Edith began to shed the layers of guilt and helplessness that had weighed her down. She learned practical coping strategies, like setting boundaries and asking for help. "You don't have to do everything yourself," Dr. Patel reminded her. "It's okay to lean on others."

One sunny afternoon, Edith decided to put her newfound insights into practice. She approached Roseanne, who was playing quietly with her dolls. "How about we have a fun art day?" she suggested, a genuine smile breaking through her earlier gloom.

"Really? That sounds awesome!" Roseanne exclaimed, her eyes lighting up.

As they set up the table with paints and brushes, Edith felt a sense of joy she hadn't experienced in months. "Let's paint a picture of our favorite place," she suggested. "I want to paint the beach!" Roseanne declared, her enthusiasm infectious.

As they painted, laughter filled the room, and for the first time in a long while, Edith felt the heaviness begin to lift. "Mom, look at my waves!" Roseanne giggled, showing off her colorful strokes.

"They're beautiful, just like you," Edith replied, her heart swelling with love.

Days turned into weeks, and with the support of therapy and her daughter's laughter, Edith began to reclaim her life. She started to reconnect with friends, accepting invitations to coffee and sharing her journey.

"You're doing so much better, Edith!" Laura exclaimed during one of their catch-ups. "It's wonderful to see you smile again."

"I've learned that it's okay to ask for help," Edith admitted, a newfound confidence in her voice. "And I'm learning to take care of myself, too."

As Roseanne's health fluctuated, Edith remained steadfast but now equipped with tools to manage her emotions. "I'm here for you, Mom," Roseanne said one evening, noticing the sparkle returning to her mother's eyes.

"And I'm here for you, sweetheart. We're a team," Edith replied, pulling her daughter into a warm embrace.

In the months that followed, Edith found a rhythm. She still faced challenges, but her perspective had shifted. "Every day is a new opportunity," she told Roseanne as they settled into their evening routine.

"Even when things are hard?" Roseanne asked, her voice small. "Especially then," Edith replied, her heart full. "Those are the days that remind us how strong we really are."

With each passing day, Edith embraced her role as a caregiver while honoring her own needs. She painted, she laughed, and she allowed herself to feel joy again, even in the midst of adversity.

As the sun set on another day, Edith reflected on her journey. "I may not have all the answers, but I'm learning," she murmured to herself. And in that moment, she knew she was not just surviving; she was truly living, one day at a time.

Depression can have a number of negative effects on a caregiver, particularly if they are caring for someone with a chronic illness or disability.

Some potential effects of depression on a caregiver include:

Increased stress and anxiety: Depression can make it more difficult for a caregiver to manage their own stress and anxiety levels, which may already be high due to the demands of caregiving.

Reduced quality of life: Caregiving can be emotionally and physically draining. Depression can make it more difficult for a caregiver to find joy in their daily life and may lead to feelings of isolation and loneliness.

Physical health problems: Depression can weaken the immune system and increase the risk of developing physical health problems, such as chronic pain, heart disease, and diabetes. Caregivers who are already at risk for these conditions may be more vulnerable to their effects.

Reduced ability to provide care: If a caregiver is struggling with depression, they may have less energy and motivation to provide the level of care that their loved one needs.

Increased risk of burnout: Caregivers who are struggling with depression may be more likely to experience burnout, which can lead to feelings of exhaustion, frustration, and resentment.

It is common for caregivers to experience feelings of depression especially if they are providing care for a loved one with a chronic or terminal illness.

Overall, depression can have a significant impact on a caregiver to provide effective care and maintain their own physical and emotional well-being. It is important for caregivers to seek support and treatment if they are struggling with depression.

Here are some tips that may help if you are feeling depressed while caregiving:

Take care of yourself: It's important to prioritize your own physical and emotional well-being. Make sure you are getting enough sleep, eating a healthy diet, and exercising regularly.

Seek support: Talk to a therapist, counselor, or support group to help you cope with your feelings. It can be helpful to speak with someone who understands what you are going through and can offer guidance.

Set boundaries: It's important to set boundaries and prioritize your own needs. Don't be afraid to ask for help, delegate tasks, or take breaks when you need them.

Practice self-care: Engage in activities that you enjoy and that help you relax, such as reading, listening to music, or taking a bath. Make time for yourself, even if it's just a few minutes a day.

Seek professional help: If your feelings of depression persist or become overwhelming, it may be helpful to speak with a mental health professional. They can provide you with additional resources and support.

Remember, it's important to take care of yourself so that you can continue to provide the best care possible to your loved one.

The Importance of Strengthening Your Mental Health

Good mental health in full-time caregivers refers to a state of well-being where the caregiver is able to effectively manage the physical, emotional, and psychological demands of their caregiving role. This includes being able to cope with stress, maintain a positive outlook, and have a sense of purpose and fulfillment in their caregiving work.

Some indicators of good mental health in full-time caregivers may include:

Resilience: The ability to bounce back from difficult situations and maintain a positive outlook, even in the face of stress and adversity.

Emotional balance: The ability to manage and regulate emotions, such as anger, frustration, and sadness, in a healthy and constructive way.

Self-care: The ability to prioritize self-care activities, such as exercise, relaxation, and socializing, which help maintain physical and mental well-being.

Social support: The presence of a strong social support network, whether it be through friends, family, or support groups, which can provide emotional and practical assistance when needed.

Sense of purpose: A sense of fulfillment and purpose in their caregiving role, with a clear understanding of how their work is making a positive impact on the lives of those they are caring for.

Overall, good mental health in full-time caregivers involves a combination of personal resilience, supportive relationships, and a sense of purpose and fulfillment in their caregiving work.

Why Mental Health Is Essential for Caregivers

Full-time caregivers often provide their loved ones with almost constant care, leaving little time for themselves. Indeed, it is not uncommon for caregivers to neglect their own mental health during this process. Caregiving can be emotionally taxing, and if a caregiver is not prioritizing their mental health, they may find themselves facing burnout, depression and anxiety.

Common Mental Health Struggles for Caregivers

Caregivers are more likely to suffer from depression and anxiety than most other people. They can experience symptoms of trauma such as anxiety, depression, and difficulty sleeping. Studies have also shown that they may have a higher risk of suicide. These issues are largely due to the demands of caregiving alone, and the additional physical and emotional stressors that often come with it, including grief over the loss of the person they are caring for, financial strain, and social isolation.

Why Mental Health Is Stigmatized Among Caregivers

Mental illness is still stigmatized in many societies, and this stigma is not limited only to professionals. People often assume that because caregivers are providing care and support to their loved ones, they should be able to handle the emotional burden without additional support. This stigma can make caregivers less willing to seek help, which can worsen already established symptoms and potentially delay or prevent treatment.

The Benefits of Seeking Mental Health Support

Getting emotional support can help caregivers avoid burnout, depression, and anxiety. It can also assist them in leading a more balanced and fulfilling life as caregivers, reduce the risk of developing depression, and improving overall life satisfaction. Moreover, caregivers can benefit from discussing the challenges they face, identifying their emotions and prioritizing self-care.

How to Prioritize Your Mental Health

The first step in prioritizing mental health is to recognize that it is essential. Caregivers should set aside time for themselves every day, whether it's taking a walk, reading, or practicing yoga, as this can help them to unwind and relax. Additionally, pursuing a hobby or joining a social group can help to combat social isolation, which can be a significant issue for caregivers.

As a caregiver, it's crucial to understand that prioritizing your own mental health is not merely a luxury; it is an absolute necessity. The demands of caregiving can be overwhelming, often leading to stress, burnout, and emotional fatigue. However, recognizing the importance of self-care is essential for both your well-being and the quality of care you provide to those you support.

It can be challenging to prioritize your own needs amid the demands of caregiving. The instinct to prioritize the well-being of those in your care often leads caregivers to overlook their own health. When you take time to care for yourself—whether through mindfulness practices, regular exercise, or simply taking a break to relax—you are not being selfish; you are ensuring that you can continue to provide high-quality care.

Being kind to yourself is fundamental. Acknowledge your feelings, no matter how complex they may be. Give yourself permission to feel overwhelmed, anxious, or even frustrated. Seeking support is also essential; whether it's confiding in friends, joining a caregiver support group, or seeking professional help, connecting with others who understand your experience can provide relief and perspective.

Staying connected with friends and family is another vital aspect of maintaining your mental health. Isolation can exacerbate feelings of stress and burnout. Sharing your experiences, joys, and challenges with others can foster a sense of community and belonging, which is invaluable during difficult times. Remember, taking care of yourself is the foundation for effective caregiving.

Coping with Everyday Challenges: A Mindful Approach to Self-Care

Understanding the Importance of Self-Care

When taking care of another person, it can be easy to forget about your own needs. However, self-care is crucial for full-time caregivers to prevent burnout, maintain good physical and mental health, and provide better care for their loved ones. Self-care can take many forms, including exercise, hobbies, social activities, and relaxation techniques.

Mindful Self-Care Techniques

Incorporating mindfulness into self-care practice can be particularly helpful for full-time caregivers. Mindfulness is the practice of paying attention to the present moment without judgment. This can help caregivers to manage their stress better, stay focused, and preserve their emotional energy.

Mindful breathing is a simple yet effective technique for reducing stress and promoting relaxation. To practice mindful breathing, sit comfortably and focus your attention on your breath. Take deep inhales and exhales, counting to 4 on the inhale and 6 on the exhale. Repeat as necessary and notice the sensations in your body with each breath.

Mindful movement is another effective self-care technique for full-time caregivers. Yoga or other gentle exercises can help caregivers release tension, increase flexibility, and reduce stress. Yoga poses like cat-cow, downward dog, and child's pose can be particularly beneficial for caregivers.

Other Self-Care Strategies

There are many other self-care strategies that caregivers can utilize to manage everyday challenges. Maintaining a healthy diet and staying hydrated is crucial for physical and mental wellbeing. Getting enough sleep is also important for managing stress and preventing burnout. Engaging in hobbies and activities that bring joy and relaxation can help caregivers to recharge and stay motivated.

Social support is also a critical aspect of self-care for full-time caregivers. Connecting with others who are going through similar experiences can provide emotional validation and reduce feelings of isolation. Joining a caregiver support group or seeking therapy can be helpful for building a support network.

Overcoming Barriers to Self-Care

Despite the many benefits of self-care, it can be challenging for full-time caregivers to make time for themselves. Caregivers may feel guilty or selfish for taking time away from their loved ones, or they may face logistical barriers such as lack of time or resources. It is important for caregivers to recognize that self-care is not a luxury, but a necessity for their own wellbeing and the quality of care they are able to provide.

One approach to overcoming barriers to self-care is to break tasks down into manageable steps. This can involve setting small goals for self-care activities, such as taking a 10-minute walk, meditating for 5 minutes, or scheduling a social outing once a week. Caregivers can also delegate responsibilities to family members or hire respite care to provide them time for self-care.

Self-care is a vital component of the caregiving experience. Mindful self-care techniques, healthy habits, social support, and overcoming barriers can all help caregivers to manage everyday challenges and prevent burnout. By taking care of themselves, caregivers can provide better care for their loved ones and maintain their own wellbeing.

Turning Pain Into Purpose

At just 25 years old, Maria had traversed a path filled with challenges that many would find overwhelming. Growing up in a small mountain village, she was no stranger to hardship. Her father had passed away when she was a young child, leaving her mother to raise Maria and her two younger siblings alone. Despite the weight of these struggles, Maria embodied kindness and compassion—a heart brimming with love and a steadfast desire to help others.

After high school, Maria set her sights on the city, driven by her dream of becoming a nurse. The transition was daunting. "I remember standing at the bus station, clutching my backpack, thinking, 'What am I doing?'" she recalled during a conversation with a close friend. But she was determined. She worked tirelessly to earn her nursing degree, balancing late-night study sessions and part-time jobs.

Her hard work paid off when she landed a job at a local hospital. It was there that she met Mrs. Wilson, an elderly woman whose warmth radiated even in the sterile confines of the hospital room. Mrs. Wilson had been admitted for treatment of a serious illness, and Maria was immediately drawn to her gentle spirit.

"I've seen a lot of nurses come and go, but you... you have a special touch," Mrs. Wilson said one day, her voice soft but sincere. Maria felt a rush of warmth at the compliment. Their connection blossomed quickly, with Maria spending hours by Mrs. Wilson's bedside, sharing stories and laughter amidst the backdrop of medical machinery and beeping monitors.

As Mrs. Wilson's condition worsened, Maria felt a deepening sense of responsibility. "I can't just sit here and watch her suffer. I need to do more," she confided to her colleague, Sarah, during a break. Driven by this conviction, Maria began volunteering her time outside of work. She would visit Mrs. Wilson at her home, bringing homemade meals and companionship, offering solace in the face of the inevitable.

Weeks turned into months, and it became clear that Maria's role was evolving. "You've become like a daughter to me," Mrs. Wilson said one afternoon, her frail hand grasping Maria's tightly. Those words resonated deeply with Maria, igniting a fierce commitment to her friend. Soon, Maria became Mrs. Wilson's full-time caregiver, dedicating herself entirely to providing the best possible care.

Maria's days were filled with tasks that were both physically demanding and emotionally taxing. She cooked for Mrs. Wilson, helped her bathe and dress, and provided companionship—sometimes simply sitting in silence, holding her hand during moments of pain. "You make this easier," Mrs. Wilson would whisper, her eyes filled with gratitude. Maria never complained, even on the hardest days when exhaustion pressed down on her like a heavy blanket.

MARIA POURED HER HEART INTO CARING FOR OTHERS.

As Mrs. Wilson's health continued to decline, Maria prepared herself for the inevitable. She often found herself reflecting on the life lessons she learned from her friend. "You taught me that kindness is a strength," Maria said during one of their many heartfelt conversations. Mrs. Wilson smiled weakly, her eyes sparkling despite the pain. "And you, my dear, are the embodiment of that strength."

When the day came that Mrs. Wilson passed away, Maria was devastated. She had lost not only a dear friend but someone who had become family. "I didn't just care for her; I loved her," Maria admitted tearfully to Sarah later. "It felt like losing a part of myself."

Yet, even in the depths of her grief, Maria found solace in knowing she had done everything she could to make Mrs. Wilson's final days comfortable and peaceful. "I can't change what happened, but I can honor her memory by helping others," she concluded, her resolve strengthening.

In the months that followed, Maria poured her heart into caring for others, driven by the lessons learned from Mrs. Wilson. She volunteered at a hospice, where she provided care and support to patients nearing the end of their lives. Each interaction was imbued with the love she had shared with Mrs. Wilson. "Every moment matters," she would tell her patients, drawing from her own experiences.

Maria also became an active member of her community, organizing events and programs to help those in need. "We need to lift each other up," she often said during planning meetings. Her unwavering dedication inspired others to join her efforts, creating a ripple effect of kindness throughout the community.

One day, while organizing a fundraiser for local families in need, Maria's friend Lisa approached her. "You know, Maria, you've turned your pain into purpose. It's incredible to see how you've transformed your grief into something beautiful." Maria smiled, her heart swelling with gratitude. "I just want to make a difference, one person at a time."

Throughout it all, Maria remained a kind and compassionate caregiver, steadfast in her belief that her role was crucial. She never allowed herself to feel guilty or ashamed for the love and care she provided. "I'm doing something important. I'm making a real difference," she would remind herself during moments of doubt.

And in the end, which was all that truly mattered to her. In a world that often seemed chaotic and unforgiving, Maria found her purpose in the quiet, profound act of caring for others. "Life is about connections," she often mused. "And I want to make every connection count."

As she continued her journey, Maria understood that her experiences had shaped her into the caregiver she had always aspired to be—one who carried the legacy of love forward, ensuring that no one faced their final days alone. In her heart, she knew that Mrs. Wilson was watching over her, proud of the woman she had become.

Frequently Asked Questions:

What are some common causes of depression in caregivers?
Giving up a career or social life, lack of support, and financial pressure are some common causes of depression in caregivers.

Can taking care of a loved one cause depression?
Yes, taking care of a loved one can lead to depression, especially if the caregiver feels overwhelmed, isolated, and unsupported.

What are some self-care strategies for caregivers dealing with depression?
Self-care strategies for caregivers dealing with depression include regular exercise, eating healthy, getting enough sleep, and practicing mindfulness.

Is it common for full-time caregivers to feel isolated and overwhelmed?
Yes, it's common for full-time caregivers to feel isolated and overwhelmed, given the challenging demands of caregiving.

When is it best to seek professional help for depression as a caregiver?
Caregivers should seek professional help for depression as soon as possible if they experience suicidal ideation, loss of interest in activities, difficulty in taking care of themselves and the people they are caring for, or if their depression is affecting their daily functioning.

CHAPTER 4 — WHEN CAREGIVING ENDS

HOW TO TRANSITION TO A NEW LIFE AS A FORMER FULL-TIME CAREGIVER

When caring for a loved one who is ill or aging, it is a natural instinct to focus on their needs and wellbeing. However, it is important to remember that caregiving comes with a definitive end. Eventually, the care recipient will pass away or transition to a long-term care facility. Preparing for this end can be challenging, but it is an essential part of the caregiving journey. We'll discuss how to smoothly transition from a caregiver to a free person again and suggest some things to consider and steps to take.

Understanding the End-of-Life Process

One of the most critical aspects of preparing for the end of caregiving is understanding the end-of-life process. Often, caregivers and their loved ones avoid discussing death and what to expect during this time. However, having an honest and open conversation about death and the dying process can be beneficial for all involved.

For instance, discussing the type of care the care recipient would like towards the end of their life helps ensure their wishes are respected. It also helps in preparing the caregiver emotionally, mentally, and practically.

The Emotions of Ending Caregiving

Caregiving can be a fulfilling experience that turns into an intimate connection between the caregiver and the patient. Losing that connection can bring a variety of emotions. Many caregivers report feeling a sense of loss or grief, disorientation, or even guilt that they are feeling relief. These are all normal emotions that you may experience during this time of transition. You don't have to go through them alone.

The First Steps

One of the most practical steps is to set up a support system before caregiving ends. Preparing to transition can be overwhelming, and having someone to rely on can ease the burden. Talk to your support network about what you currently need and how they can help. It may be helpful to seek counseling to navigate the complex emotional landscape.

Things to Consider

Remember that your identity as a caregiver doesn't define you. You have unique skills and qualities that can be channeled into other areas of your life beyond caregiving. Take some time to assess what matters to you- are there any passions or hobbies that you had to put on hold during caregiving? Focus on returning to those pursuits and building a new life and routine beyond caregiving.

Coping with Insensitive Suggestions

It is difficult to overstate the importance of having a supportive network. However, there are times when loved ones, family members, or friends may offer insensitive advice or suggestions.

Regrettably, some of these suggestions can go so far as to blame you for becoming a caregiver in the first place or undermine your experience of caring for another person. It is important to remember that these individuals may not fully comprehend the emotional and physical effort involved in caregiving.

Taking Care of Yourself

Caregiving is a demanding job that can take a toll on the caregiver's physical and emotional health. As the end of caregiving approaches, it is even more critical to prioritize self-care.

Taking the time to exercise, eat healthily, and get enough sleep can help caregivers maintain their physical health. It is also essential to take breaks and engage in enjoyable activities to prevent emotional exhaustion and burnout.

Managing Practical Matters

In addition to taking care of themselves emotionally and physically, caregivers must also consider the practicalities that come with the end of caregiving. For many caregivers, the end of full-time care brings changes to their financial situation. It may be worthwhile to consult with a financial advisor or lawyer to ensure you are taking advantage of everything your loved one is eligible for during end-of-life planning. Make sure everything is organized and that you know what steps to take.

Additionally, caregivers may need to prepare the care recipient's home for sale or consider assisted living options. Taking care of these practical matters well in advance can help to alleviate stress and prevent last-minute decisions.

Practicing Self-Compassion

Finally, practicing self-compassion is a crucial component of preparing for the end of caregiving. Caregivers often feel a sense of guilt or a lack of fulfillment as their role comes to an end. It is essential to recognize that these feelings are normal and that caregivers should practice self-compassion rather than judgement.

This may mean embracing the emotions that come with closure, focusing on the positive memories and moments shared with the care recipient, and finding new ways to give back to the community.

Tips for a Smooth Transition

• **Take Baby Steps:** Give yourself time to adjust, this can be a massive adjustment for you.

• **Don't be too hard on Yourself:** You did the best you could to help your loved one. Don't regret things you couldn't do.

• **Take Care of Yourself:** It's essential to take this time to focus on your health: visit your doctor, eat well, exercise, and find mental clarity doing activities you enjoy.

• **Seek Out Your Interests:** Reconnect with friends or find local groups that match your interests.

• **Volunteer:** You can volunteer with seniors or volunteer with animals or a cause that you feel passionate about.

A New Chapter

The soft hum of the intercom echoed through the house, a lifeline between Myron and his mother, Marlene. "Myron," her voice crackled through, weary but warm, "can you bring me the remote? I can't reach it."

"Coming, Mom!" he called back, striding up the stairs. He paused at her bedroom door, taking a moment to collect himself. This was the routine now—fetching, caring, and listening. But today felt different. As he entered, he was greeted by the familiar sight of her frail figure nestled against the pillows, the wide-screen TV casting a soft glow across her face.

"Thanks, sweetie," she said, her eyes brightening as he handed her the remote. "What are we watching today?"

"Just the news. I thought you might want to catch up," he replied, settling into the chair beside her bed. He forced a smile, even as worry gnawed at him. "You know, they say there's a storm coming."

Marlene chuckled lightly, a sound that reminded Myron of the days when she would sweep him up into her arms after a fall, making everything feel alright. "A little rain won't hurt us. Just a bit of water on the garden."

As he watched her, he felt a familiar ache in his chest. The reality of her failing health was an ever-present shadow, growing darker with each passing day. The hospice team had become a regular part of their lives, with nurses like Kristen showing up with warmth and compassion.

Just then, a gentle knock interrupted his thoughts. The door opened to reveal Kristen, the hospice nurse, her demeanor calm and reassuring. "Hello, Marlene! How are we doing today?"

"Like a daisy in the sun," Marlene replied, her tone teasing, even as it was laced with fatigue.

Kristen smiled, the kind of smile that could light up a room. "I love that spirit! Let's check your vitals, shall we?" She moved deftly, her hands practiced and gentle. "Myron, how are you holding up?"

"I'm fine," he insisted, though the weariness in his voice betrayed him.

Kristen raised an eyebrow, a knowing look passing between them. "You need to remember to take care of yourself too, Myron. It's not just about Marlene."

"I know," he said, though he felt a swell of guilt. "It's just… it's hard to think about anything else right now."

At that moment, Joshua, the hospice chaplain, entered, his presence a calming effect in the room. "Good afternoon, everyone. Mind if I join?"

"Of course, Joshua," Kristen said, her smile widening. "We could use some of your wisdom."

"Wisdom? Or just a listening ear?" Joshua replied, settling into the chair next to Myron.

"Today is a good day to talk about what's on your mind, Myron."

Myron sighed, feeling a wave of vulnerability wash over him. "It's just… I've been so focused on taking care of Mom that I haven't thought about my own life. What comes next?"

Joshua nodded understandingly. "It's not uncommon for caregivers to feel this way. You've poured your heart into caring for Marlene. But you also have dreams, Myron."

"Dreams?" Myron echoed, shaking his head. "I used to dream of travel, of writing novels. Now I can barely think beyond the next meal or the next appointment."

"Have you talked to anyone about this?" Joshua asked gently.

"I spoke to Rev. Weldon," Myron admitted. "He helped with Mom's arrangements, but… I haven't really thought about what I want."

"Maybe it's time to start," Kristen interjected, her voice encouraging. "You deserve happiness too, Myron. It's okay to plan for your future."

"But what if I'm wishing her away?" he said, his voice trembling. "I don't want to feel like I'm abandoning her."

Marlene reached out, her frail hand resting on his arm. "Myron, my dear," she said softly, "you've done everything for me. I want you to live your life, to chase those dreams. I won't hold you back."

Tears brimmed in Myron's eyes. "Mom… I just don't know how."

"Start small," Joshua suggested. "Think about one thing you'd like to do—something that brings you joy."

After a moment, Myron spoke, the words tumbling out. "I've always wanted to go to Barbados. I have friends there, and I've thought about it for years."

"Then plan it," Kristen said, her eyes sparkling with enthusiasm. "Why not speak to a travel agent? You could use a getaway."

"I could," Myron murmured, the idea sparking a flicker of hope within him. "But what about the guilt?"

"Guilt is a heavy burden," Joshua said. "You have to find balance. It's not selfish to want to live your life."

Marlene's voice was steady, filled with love. "Promise me you'll think about it, Myron. I'll be okay knowing you're taking care of yourself too."

As the conversation continued, Myron felt a shift within himself. He began to envision the possibilities—Barbados, an Alaskan cruise, maybe even taking saxophone lessons again. The thought of reviving his passion felt like a breath of fresh air.

In the days that followed, he reached out to Kenisha Tucker at VIP Travel Escape, and together they mapped out adventures that reignited the spark of hope within him. It was a tentative step, but one filled with promise.

Marlene's health continued to decline, but her transition was peaceful, surrounded by love and the support of the hospice team. In her final moments, she squeezed Myron's hand, her eyes reflecting gratitude. "Thank you, Myron. You've made my life beautiful."

After her passing, Myron felt the weight of loss, but he also felt lighter, as if a new chapter was beginning. He embraced the journey ahead, honoring his mother's memory by living fully.

As he sat down to write his first novel, he could almost hear her voice, encouraging him, saying, "Go on, Myron. Live."

Ten Steps to Prepare for the End:

Preparing for the end of life of a loved one can be an emotionally challenging process.

Here are some steps that may help:

1. Open Communication: Encourage honest conversations about feelings, fears, and wishes. Discuss end-of-life preferences, including hospice care and advanced directives.

2. Understand Their Wishes: Make sure you know their desires regarding medical treatment, living arrangements, and final wishes. This can include preferences for pain management and any specific requests for their care.

3. Create a Support Network: Surround yourself and your loved one with supportive family and friends. This network can provide emotional and practical assistance during this time.

4. Explore Hospice and Palliative Care: Consider involving hospice or palliative care services. These professionals can provide comfort, pain relief, and support for both the patient and the family.

5. Organize Important Documents: Gather essential documents like wills, insurance policies, and medical records. This makes it easier to manage affairs as needed.

6. Take Care of Yourself: Caring for a loved one can be overwhelming. Make sure to prioritize your own health and well-being. Seek support from friends, family, or professional counselors if necessary.

7. Create Lasting Memories: Spend quality time together and create meaningful experiences. This can be through storytelling, revisiting favorite activities, or simply being present.

8. Consider Spiritual Needs: If applicable, discuss spiritual beliefs and wishes. Involvement of spiritual leaders or counselors can provide comfort.

9. Plan for After Their Passing: Discuss and plan for arrangements that may need to be made after their passing, such as funerals or memorial services.

10. Be Present: Sometimes, simply being there and listening is the most comforting thing you can offer. Let them know they are loved and supported.

Each situation is unique, so adapt these suggestions to fit the specific needs and circumstances of your loved one and family.

As you approach the conclusion of your caregiving journey, navigating this transition can feel daunting. However, by familiarizing yourself with the end-of-life process, establishing a robust support network, prioritizing self-care, and embracing self-compassion, you can alleviate stress and prevent burnout. Remember, taking care of your physical and emotional well-being is essential during this challenging time.

We hope this guide has illuminated the often-overlooked emotions and challenges faced by full-time caregivers. We have delved into the emotional turmoil they experience, the stigma surrounding their mental health needs, and the daily obstacles they encounter.

Importantly, we've highlighted the necessity of self-care and the advantages of cultivating a strong support system. Recognizing the invaluable role caregivers play in our communities—through their personal sacrifices and the profound impact they have on their loved ones' lives—is crucial. The insights shared in this guide aim to empower caregivers to confront their emotional struggles and prioritize their mental wellness.

We trust that the information provided will serve as a valuable resource, helping caregivers adopt a mindful approach to combat feelings of loneliness, abandonment, and depression while fostering supportive communities. In doing so, caregivers can enhance their well-being and provide even better care. Ultimately, we aspire for this guide to contribute to a healthier, more supportive environment for all caregivers.

Frequently Asked Questions:

How long will it take to transition from a life of caregiving to a new routine?

While every situation is different, it is common for caregivers to take several months or even a year to transition smoothly.

How do I deal with the guilt of feeling relieved that my caregiving responsibilities have ended?

It is natural to experience some relief that your caregiving journey has ended, but it is also common to feel guilty about it. Speaking with a counselor or someone in your support network can help you process those emotions.

Who should I consult with if caregiving has financially impacted me?

Consulting with a financial advisor or a lawyer is an excellent step to help understand your unique financial situation and any benefits you or your loved one are entitled to.

How do I cope with insensitive suggestions from family and friends who have never been caregivers?

Remember that those individuals may not have a full understanding of what you've gone through. Focusing on your support network and what works best for you can help you find stability in times of emotional stress.

How do I start reconnecting with my passions or hobbies after caregiving ends?

Taking small steps, such as contacting old friends, diving into hobbies, and volunteering, can help reignite your passions and interests and find meaning outside of caregiving.

Caregivers Bill of Rights

The Components of the Caregiver's Bill of Rights

The Caregiver's Bill of Rights is made up of five components that empower caregivers to take care of themselves while providing care to their loved ones.

These rights include:

• **Right to Self-Care**

Caregivers have a right to take care of their physical and emotional health needs. Taking care of yourself is essential to ensure that you remain healthy and are capable of providing care in the long-term.

• Right to Seek Assistance

Taking care of someone with a health issue or disability can be challenging, and caregivers need to have access to resources and support when they need it. This right provides caregivers with the opportunity to seek assistance from family members, medical professionals, and community resources.

• Right to Balance

Caregiving can be a full-time job, and it's essential to achieve a balance between your responsibilities as a caregiver and your personal life. This right encourages caregivers to seek out activities that bring them joy and fulfillment outside of caregiving.

• Right to Respect

Caregivers have a right to respect from their loved ones and medical professionals. Their opinions and views on the care of their loved ones should be considered when creating care plans.

• Right to Information

Caregivers need to have access to information about their loved ones' medical condition and care plan. This right encourages healthcare professionals to provide caregivers with information that will help them provide the best care possible.

How the Caregiver's Bill of Rights Can Improve Caregiving

Implementing the Caregiver's Bill of Rights can improve caregiving in several ways, including:

Improving Overall Health and Well being

Caregivers who practice self-care and seek assistance when needed are more likely to remain healthy and avoid burnout.

Improved Caregiver-Recipient Relationship

Caregivers who have access to resources and support are better equipped to provide quality care to their loved ones, improving the caregiver-recipient relationship.

Reduced Caregiver Burnout and Stress

Taking care of your physical and emotional health needs can reduce stress and burnout, making caregiving more manageable in the long-term.

The Caregiver's Bill of Rights provides a framework that supports family caregivers and promotes their rights to take care of themselves while caring for their loved ones. These rights can improve care recipients' health outcomes, improve caregiver recipient relationships, and reduce caregiver stress and burnout.

If you are a caregiver, make sure you familiarize yourself with these rights, and don't be afraid to advocate for your needs. By taking care of yourself, you can provide better care for your loved ones.

Maximizing the Guide into your Journey

To maximize this guide, we recommend:

- Dedicate regular time to reflect on the information and your experiences.

- Use the guide as a resource for support.

- Connect with support groups or online communities for encouragement.

- Celebrate small victories and acknowledge your growth.

Remember, overcoming loneliness, abandonment and depression is a gradual process. Be patient with yourself, practice self-compassion, and utilize the resources to enhance your mental health and overall well-being.

My hope is that this guide has illuminated the emotional struggles of full-time caregivers. In this guide, I've explored the causes and effects of loneliness, abandonment and depression with suggestions for overcoming them.

The importance of self-care is emphasized, and I recognize the vital role caregivers play in our society. The insights shared here aim to empower caregivers to address their emotional challenges and prioritize mental health.

This guide serves as a resource for adopting a mindful approach to self-care and fostering supportive communities, helping caregivers improve their well-being and care for their loved ones. We aspire for this work to contribute to a healthier society for caregivers.

"CAREGIVERS DO MATTER."

www.**Moore**BooksR.us

OVERCOMING...

A Caregiver's Guide

Explore the emotional struggles and challenges faced by full-time caregivers, delving into the causes, effects, and strategies for overcoming feelings of frustration, anger, stress, guilt and exhaustion. These guides also underscore the vital importance of self-care.

It is essential to acknowledge the immense role that caregivers play in our society, highlighting their personal sacrifices and the profound impact they have on the lives of those they care for. The knowledge shared will serve as a guide for caregivers to embrace a mindful approach to self-care and cultivate supportive communities, fostering improved well-being and enhanced care for their loved ones.

The ultimate goal of this book is to contribute to a healthier, more compassionate society that values the crucial work of caregivers.

Remember, *Caregivers DO Matter.*

OVERCOMING

- Frustration, Anger, & Exhaustion
- Loneliness, Abandonment,
  & Depression
- Anxiety, Worry, & Stress
- Guilt. Grief, & Regret

www.MooreBooksR.us

Think Feel Speak Write — Do 2.0

A Path Toward Realizing Your Purpose

Many of us are frustrated, confused, and lack enthusiasm; just going through the motions in life. We have settled for the world's definition of who we are instead of agreeing with God who has created us on purpose.

In this book are insights and stories that offer a fresh outlook on how these principles can impact your journey. You too may find that as you Think, Feel, Speak, Write, and DO purposefully, you can live a fulfilling life as God created you to live, with purpose.

Get started today!

www.onecreativemindllc.com/think2 or thinkfeelspeakwritedo2.com

---

"Why Won't They Just Die!"

"Emotional turmoil of Caregivers often goes unnoticed."

When a caregiver experiences the thought, "why won't they just die!" they are not actually expressing a wish for the death of their loved one. It's used in a time when the caregiver feels that they've reached their limit; in a moment of over-whelm, frustration and desperation, where they feel like they're running out of options.

www.whywonttheyjustdie.com

Contact R. Lee Moore, Sr.

For Book Signings &
Speaking Engagements:

RLeeMooreSr@gmail.com

(844) 246-2200

www.RonaldLeeMooreSr.com

R. Lee Moore, Sr.
295 E. Swedesford Road, #288
Wayne, PA 19087

www.**Moore**BooksR.us